ESTD 2020

MY HOME BREWING

RECIPE JOURNAL

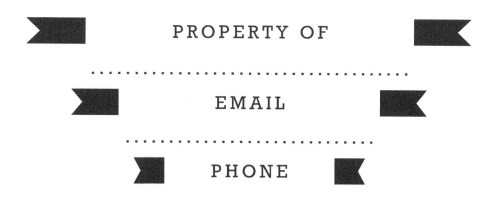

PROPERTY OF

....

EMAIL

....

PHONE

....

facebook.com/BrewingJournals

INDEX OF RECIPES

BATCH NO.	BEER NAME	STYLE	FAV	PAGE
			☆	6
			☆	8
			☆	10
			☆	12
			☆	14
			☆	16
			☆	18
			☆	20
			☆	22
			☆	24
			☆	26
			☆	28
			☆	30
			☆	32
			☆	34
			☆	36
			☆	38
			☆	40
			☆	42
			☆	44
			☆	46
			☆	48
			☆	50
			☆	52
			☆	54
			☆	56
			☆	58
			☆	60
			☆	62
			☆	64

INDEX OF RECIPES

BEER INFO		RATING:	☆ ☆ ☆ ☆ ☆

BEER NAME .... BATCH NO. ....

STYLE .... BATCH VOLUME ....

BREWER .... DATE ....

OG		FG		ABV		SRM		IBU	
EXPECTED	ACTUAL								

GRAIN	AMT.
TOTAL	

HOPS		FORM	AA	IBU	TIME	AMT.
		TOTAL				

WATER TREATMENTS	pH		AMT.

YEAST STRAIN	AMT.

OTHER INGREDIENTS	AMT.

BREWING					
TIME	STEP	[STRIKE, MASH-IN, MASH-OUT, SPARGE, BOIL, KNOCKOUT]	TEMP	VOLUME	GRAVITY
	1.				
	2.				
	3.				
	4.				
	5.				
	6.				

FERMENTATION					
DATE	STEP		START TEMP	END TEMP	GRAVITY	DAYS
	1.				
	2.				
	3.				
	4.				

FERMENTATION ADDITIONS

DATE	ADDITION	AMT.	DAYS

PACKAGING

DATE	FINAL VOLUME	NUMBER OF BOTTLES	NUMBER OF KEGS	READY TO DRINK BY DATE

INGREDIENTS INFORMATION

....
....
....
....
....
....
....

BREWING NOTES

....
....
....
....
....
....
....

TASTING NOTES

ADDITIONAL INFORMATION

UNITS OF MEASUREMENT	
TEMP	
WEIGHT	
VOLUME	

BEER INFO						RATING:	☆ ☆ ☆ ☆ ☆

BEER NAME .... **BATCH NO.** ....

STYLE .... **BATCH VOLUME** ....

BREWER .... **DATE** ....

OG		FG		ABV		SRM		IBU	
EXPECTED	ACTUAL								

GRAIN	AMT.
TOTAL	

HOPS	FORM	AA	IBU	TIME	AMT.
TOTAL					

WATER TREATMENTS	pH		AMT.

YEAST STRAIN	AMT.

OTHER INGREDIENTS	AMT.

BREWING					
TIME	STEP	[STRIKE, MASH-IN, MASH-OUT, SPARGE, BOIL, KNOCKOUT]	TEMP	VOLUME	GRAVITY
	1.				
	2.				
	3.				
	4.				
	5.				
	6.				

FERMENTATION					
DATE	STEP		START TEMP	END TEMP	GRAVITY	DAYS
	1.				
	2.				
	3.				
	4.				

FERMENTATION ADDITIONS

DATE	ADDITION	AMT.	DAYS

PACKAGING

DATE	FINAL VOLUME	NUMBER OF BOTTLES	NUMBER OF KEGS	READY TO DRINK BY DATE

INGREDIENTS INFORMATION

....
....
....
....
....
....
....

BREWING NOTES

....
....
....
....
....
....
....

TASTING NOTES

ADDITIONAL INFORMATION

UNITS OF MEASUREMENT	
TEMP	
WEIGHT	
VOLUME	

BEER INFO	RATING: ☆ ☆ ☆ ☆ ☆

BEER NAME .... BATCH NO. ....

STYLE .... BATCH VOLUME ....

BREWER .... DATE ....

OG		FG		ABV		SRM		IBU	
EXPECTED	ACTUAL								

GRAIN	AMT.
TOTAL	

HOPS	FORM	AA	IBU	TIME	AMT.
TOTAL					

WATER TREATMENTS	pH		AMT.

YEAST STRAIN	AMT.

OTHER INGREDIENTS	AMT.

BREWING					
TIME	STEP	[STRIKE, MASH-IN, MASH-OUT, SPARGE, BOIL, KNOCKOUT]	TEMP	VOLUME	GRAVITY
	1.				
	2.				
	3.				
	4.				
	5.				
	6.				

FERMENTATION					
DATE	STEP		START TEMP	END TEMP	GRAVITY	DAYS
	1.					
	2.					
	3.					
	4.					

FERMENTATION ADDITIONS

DATE	ADDITION	AMT.	DAYS

PACKAGING

DATE	FINAL VOLUME	NUMBER OF BOTTLES	NUMBER OF KEGS	READY TO DRINK BY DATE

INGREDIENTS INFORMATION

....
....
....
....
....
....
....

BREWING NOTES

....
....
....
....
....
....
....

TASTING NOTES

ADDITIONAL INFORMATION

UNITS OF MEASUREMENT	
TEMP	
WEIGHT	
VOLUME	

BEER INFO	RATING: ☆ ☆ ☆ ☆ ☆

BEER NAME .... BATCH NO. ....

STYLE .... BATCH VOLUME ....

BREWER .... DATE ....

OG		FG		ABV		SRM		IBU	
EXPECTED	ACTUAL								

GRAIN	AMT.
TOTAL	

HOPS	FORM	AA	IBU	TIME	AMT.
	TOTAL				

WATER TREATMENTS	pH		AMT.

YEAST STRAIN	AMT.

OTHER INGREDIENTS	AMT.

BREWING					
TIME	STEP	[STRIKE, MASH-IN, MASH-OUT, SPARGE, BOIL, KNOCKOUT]	TEMP	VOLUME	GRAVITY
	1.				
	2.				
	3.				
	4.				
	5.				
	6.				

FERMENTATION					
DATE	STEP		START TEMP	END TEMP	GRAVITY	DAYS
	1.					
	2.					
	3.					
	4.					

FERMENTATION ADDITIONS

DATE	ADDITION	AMT.	DAYS

PACKAGING

DATE	FINAL VOLUME	NUMBER OF BOTTLES	NUMBER OF KEGS	READY TO DRINK BY DATE

INGREDIENTS INFORMATION

....
....
....
....
....
....
....

BREWING NOTES

....
....
....
....
....
....
....

TASTING NOTES

ADDITIONAL INFORMATION

UNITS OF MEASUREMENT	
TEMP	
WEIGHT	
VOLUME	

BEER INFO				RATING:	☆ ☆ ☆ ☆ ☆

BEER NAME .... BATCH NO. ....

STYLE .... BATCH VOLUME ....

BREWER .... DATE ....

OG		FG		ABV		SRM		IBU	
EXPECTED	ACTUAL								

GRAIN	AMT.
TOTAL	

HOPS	FORM	AA	IBU	TIME	AMT.
	TOTAL				

WATER TREATMENTS	pH		AMT.

YEAST STRAIN	AMT.

OTHER INGREDIENTS	AMT.

BREWING					
TIME	STEP	[STRIKE, MASH-IN, MASH-OUT, SPARGE, BOIL, KNOCKOUT]	TEMP	VOLUME	GRAVITY
	1.				
	2.				
	3.				
	4.				
	5.				
	6.				

FERMENTATION					
DATE	STEP		START TEMP	END TEMP	GRAVITY	DAYS
	1.				
	2.				
	3.				
	4.				

FERMENTATION ADDITIONS

DATE	ADDITION	AMT.	DAYS

PACKAGING

DATE	FINAL VOLUME	NUMBER OF BOTTLES	NUMBER OF KEGS	READY TO DRINK BY DATE

INGREDIENTS INFORMATION

....
....
....
....
....
....
....

BREWING NOTES

....
....
....
....
....
....
....

TASTING NOTES

ADDITIONAL INFORMATION

UNITS OF MEASUREMENT	
TEMP	
WEIGHT	
VOLUME	

BEER INFO		RATING:	☆ ☆ ☆ ☆ ☆

BEER NAME .... BATCH NO. ....

STYLE .... BATCH VOLUME ....

BREWER .... DATE ....

OG		FG	ABV	SRM	IBU
EXPECTED	ACTUAL				

GRAIN	AMT.
TOTAL	

HOPS	FORM	AA	IBU	TIME	AMT.
TOTAL					

WATER TREATMENTS	pH		AMT.

YEAST STRAIN	AMT.

OTHER INGREDIENTS	AMT.

BREWING					
TIME	STEP	[STRIKE, MASH-IN, MASH-OUT, SPARGE, BOIL, KNOCKOUT]	TEMP	VOLUME	GRAVITY
	1.				
	2.				
	3.				
	4.				
	5.				
	6.				

FERMENTATION					
DATE	STEP		START TEMP	END TEMP	GRAVITY	DAYS
	1.				
	2.				
	3.				
	4.				

FERMENTATION ADDITIONS

DATE	ADDITION	AMT.	DAYS

PACKAGING

DATE	FINAL VOLUME	NUMBER OF BOTTLES	NUMBER OF KEGS	READY TO DRINK BY DATE

INGREDIENTS INFORMATION

....

....

....

....

....

....

....

BREWING NOTES

....

....

....

....

....

....

....

TASTING NOTES

ADDITIONAL INFORMATION

UNITS OF MEASUREMENT	
TEMP	
WEIGHT	
VOLUME	

BEER INFO	RATING: ☆ ☆ ☆ ☆ ☆

BEER NAME .... BATCH NO. ....

STYLE .... BATCH VOLUME ....

BREWER .... DATE ....

OG		FG		ABV		SRM		IBU	
EXPECTED	ACTUAL								

GRAIN	AMT.
TOTAL	

HOPS		FORM	AA	IBU	TIME	AMT.
	TOTAL					

WATER TREATMENTS	pH		AMT.

OTHER INGREDIENTS	AMT.

YEAST STRAIN	AMT.

BREWING					
TIME	STEP	[STRIKE, MASH-IN, MASH-OUT, SPARGE, BOIL, KNOCKOUT]	TEMP	VOLUME	GRAVITY
	1.				
	2.				
	3.				
	4.				
	5.				
	6.				

FERMENTATION					
DATE	STEP		START TEMP	END TEMP	GRAVITY	DAYS
	1.				
	2.				
	3.				
	4.				

FERMENTATION ADDITIONS

DATE	ADDITION	AMT.	DAYS

PACKAGING

DATE	FINAL VOLUME	NUMBER OF BOTTLES	NUMBER OF KEGS	READY TO DRINK BY DATE

INGREDIENTS INFORMATION

....
....
....
....
....
....
....

BREWING NOTES

....
....
....
....
....
....
....

TASTING NOTES

ADDITIONAL INFORMATION

UNITS OF MEASUREMENT	
TEMP	
WEIGHT	
VOLUME	

BEER INFO

RATING: ☆ ☆ ☆ ☆ ☆

BEER NAME .... BATCH NO. ....

STYLE .... BATCH VOLUME ....

BREWER .... DATE ....

OG		FG		ABV		SRM		IBU	
EXPECTED	ACTUAL								

GRAIN	AMT.
TOTAL	

HOPS	FORM	AA	IBU	TIME	AMT.
TOTAL					

WATER TREATMENTS	pH		AMT.

YEAST STRAIN	AMT.

OTHER INGREDIENTS	AMT.

BREWING

TIME	STEP	[STRIKE, MASH-IN, MASH-OUT, SPARGE, BOIL, KNOCKOUT]	TEMP	VOLUME	GRAVITY
	1.				
	2.				
	3.				
	4.				
	5.				
	6.				

FERMENTATION

DATE	STEP	START TEMP	END TEMP	GRAVITY	DAYS
	1.				
	2.				
	3.				
	4.				

FERMENTATION ADDITIONS

DATE	ADDITION	AMT.	DAYS

PACKAGING

DATE	FINAL VOLUME	NUMBER OF BOTTLES	NUMBER OF KEGS	READY TO DRINK BY DATE

INGREDIENTS INFORMATION

BREWING NOTES

TASTING NOTES | ADDITIONAL INFORMATION

UNITS OF MEASUREMENT	
TEMP	
WEIGHT	
VOLUME	

BEER INFO	RATING:	☆ ☆ ☆ ☆ ☆

BEER NAME .... BATCH NO. ....

STYLE .... BATCH VOLUME ....

BREWER .... DATE ....

OG		FG		ABV		SRM		IBU	
EXPECTED	ACTUAL								

GRAIN	AMT.
TOTAL	

HOPS	FORM	AA	IBU	TIME	AMT.
TOTAL					

WATER TREATMENTS	pH		AMT.

YEAST STRAIN	AMT.

OTHER INGREDIENTS	AMT.

BREWING					
TIME	STEP	[STRIKE, MASH-IN, MASH-OUT, SPARGE, BOIL, KNOCKOUT]	TEMP	VOLUME	GRAVITY
	1.				
	2.				
	3.				
	4.				
	5.				
	6.				

FERMENTATION					
DATE	STEP		START TEMP	END TEMP	GRAVITY	DAYS
	1.				
	2.				
	3.				
	4.				

FERMENTATION ADDITIONS

DATE	ADDITION	AMT.	DAYS

PACKAGING

DATE	FINAL VOLUME	NUMBER OF BOTTLES	NUMBER OF KEGS	READY TO DRINK BY DATE

INGREDIENTS INFORMATION

....
....
....
....
....
....
....

BREWING NOTES

....
....
....
....
....
....
....

TASTING NOTES

ADDITIONAL INFORMATION

UNITS OF MEASUREMENT	
TEMP	
WEIGHT	
VOLUME	

| BEER INFO | | | | | RATING: | ☆ ☆ ☆ ☆ ☆ |

BEER NAME .... **BATCH NO.** ....

STYLE .... **BATCH VOLUME** ....

BREWER .... **DATE** ....

OG		FG		ABV		SRM		IBU	
EXPECTED	ACTUAL								

GRAIN	AMT.
TOTAL	

HOPS	FORM	AA	IBU	TIME	AMT.
			TOTAL		

WATER TREATMENTS	pH		AMT.

YEAST STRAIN	AMT.

OTHER INGREDIENTS	AMT.

BREWING

TIME	STEP	[STRIKE, MASH-IN, MASH-OUT, SPARGE, BOIL, KNOCKOUT]	TEMP	VOLUME	GRAVITY
	1.				
	2.				
	3.				
	4.				
	5.				
	6.				

FERMENTATION

DATE	STEP		START TEMP	END TEMP	GRAVITY	DAYS
	1.					
	2.					
	3.					
	4.					

FERMENTATION ADDITIONS

DATE	ADDITION	AMT.	DAYS

PACKAGING

DATE	FINAL VOLUME	NUMBER OF BOTTLES	NUMBER OF KEGS	READY TO DRINK BY DATE

INGREDIENTS INFORMATION

....

....

....

....

....

....

....

BREWING NOTES

....

....

....

....

....

....

....

TASTING NOTES

ADDITIONAL INFORMATION

UNITS OF MEASUREMENT	
TEMP	
WEIGHT	
VOLUME	

BEER INFO

RATING: ☆ ☆ ☆ ☆ ☆

BEER NAME .... BATCH NO. ....

STYLE .... BATCH VOLUME ....

BREWER .... DATE ....

OG		FG		ABV		SRM		IBU	
EXPECTED	ACTUAL								

GRAIN	AMT.
TOTAL	

HOPS	FORM	AA	IBU	TIME	AMT.
TOTAL					

WATER TREATMENTS	pH		AMT.

YEAST STRAIN	AMT.

OTHER INGREDIENTS	AMT.

BREWING

TIME	STEP	[STRIKE, MASH-IN, MASH-OUT, SPARGE, BOIL, KNOCKOUT]	TEMP	VOLUME	GRAVITY
	1.				
	2.				
	3.				
	4.				
	5.				
	6.				

FERMENTATION

DATE	STEP		START TEMP	END TEMP	GRAVITY	DAYS
	1.					
	2.					
	3.					
	4.					

FERMENTATION ADDITIONS

DATE	ADDITION	AMT.	DAYS

PACKAGING

DATE	FINAL VOLUME	NUMBER OF BOTTLES	NUMBER OF KEGS	READY TO DRINK BY DATE

INGREDIENTS INFORMATION

....
....
....
....
....
....
....

BREWING NOTES

....
....
....
....
....
....
....

TASTING NOTES

ADDITIONAL INFORMATION

UNITS OF MEASUREMENT	
TEMP	
WEIGHT	
VOLUME	

BEER INFO

RATING: ☆ ☆ ☆ ☆ ☆

BEER NAME .... BATCH NO. ....

STYLE .... BATCH VOLUME ....

BREWER .... DATE ....

OG		FG			ABV		SRM		IBU	
EXPECTED	ACTUAL									

GRAIN	AMT.
TOTAL	

HOPS	FORM	AA	IBU	TIME	AMT.
TOTAL					

WATER TREATMENTS	pH		AMT.

YEAST STRAIN	AMT.

OTHER INGREDIENTS	AMT.

BREWING

TIME	STEP [STRIKE, MASH-IN, MASH-OUT, SPARGE, BOIL, KNOCKOUT]	TEMP	VOLUME	GRAVITY
	1.			
	2.			
	3.			
	4.			
	5.			
	6.			

FERMENTATION

DATE	STEP	START TEMP	END TEMP	GRAVITY	DAYS
	1.				
	2.				
	3.				
	4.				

FERMENTATION ADDITIONS

DATE	ADDITION	AMT.	DAYS

PACKAGING

DATE	FINAL VOLUME	NUMBER OF BOTTLES	NUMBER OF KEGS	READY TO DRINK BY DATE

INGREDIENTS INFORMATION

....
....
....
....
....
....
....

BREWING NOTES

....
....
....
....
....
....
....

TASTING NOTES	ADDITIONAL INFORMATION

UNITS OF MEASUREMENT

TEMP	
WEIGHT	
VOLUME	

BEER INFO	RATING:	☆ ☆ ☆ ☆ ☆

BEER NAME .... BATCH NO. ....

STYLE .... BATCH VOLUME ....

BREWER .... DATE ....

OG		FG		ABV		SRM		IBU	
EXPECTED	ACTUAL								

GRAIN	AMT.
TOTAL	

HOPS		FORM	AA	IBU	TIME	AMT.
TOTAL						

WATER TREATMENTS	pH		AMT.

YEAST STRAIN	AMT.

OTHER INGREDIENTS	AMT.

BREWING					
TIME	STEP	[STRIKE, MASH-IN, MASH-OUT, SPARGE, BOIL, KNOCKOUT]	TEMP	VOLUME	GRAVITY
	1.				
	2.				
	3.				
	4.				
	5.				
	6.				

FERMENTATION					
DATE	STEP		START TEMP	END TEMP	GRAVITY	DAYS
	1.				
	2.				
	3.				
	4.				

FERMENTATION ADDITIONS

DATE	ADDITION	AMT.	DAYS

PACKAGING

DATE	FINAL VOLUME	NUMBER OF BOTTLES	NUMBER OF KEGS	READY TO DRINK BY DATE

INGREDIENTS INFORMATION

....
....
....
....
....
....
....

BREWING NOTES

....
....
....
....
....
....
....

TASTING NOTES

ADDITIONAL INFORMATION

UNITS OF MEASUREMENT	
TEMP	
WEIGHT	
VOLUME	

BEER INFO	RATING:	☆ ☆ ☆ ☆ ☆

BEER NAME .... BATCH NO. ....

STYLE .... BATCH VOLUME ....

BREWER .... DATE ....

OG		FG		ABV		SRM		IBU	
EXPECTED	ACTUAL								

GRAIN		AMT.
	TOTAL	

HOPS		FORM	AA	IBU	TIME	AMT.
			TOTAL		

WATER TREATMENTS	pH		AMT.

OTHER INGREDIENTS	AMT.

YEAST STRAIN	AMT.

BREWING					
TIME	STEP	[STRIKE, MASH-IN, MASH-OUT, SPARGE, BOIL, KNOCKOUT]	TEMP	VOLUME	GRAVITY
	1.				
	2.				
	3.				
	4.				
	5.				
	6.				

FERMENTATION					
DATE	STEP		START TEMP	END TEMP	GRAVITY	DAYS
	1.					
	2.					
	3.					
	4.					

FERMENTATION ADDITIONS

DATE	ADDITION	AMT.	DAYS

PACKAGING

DATE	FINAL VOLUME	NUMBER OF BOTTLES	NUMBER OF KEGS	READY TO DRINK BY DATE

INGREDIENTS INFORMATION

....
....
....
....
....
....
....

BREWING NOTES

....
....
....
....
....
....
....

TASTING NOTES

ADDITIONAL INFORMATION

UNITS OF MEASUREMENT	
TEMP	
WEIGHT	
VOLUME	

BEER INFO						RATING:	☆ ☆ ☆ ☆ ☆

BEER NAME .... BATCH NO. ....

STYLE .... BATCH VOLUME ....

BREWER .... DATE ....

OG		FG		ABV		SRM		IBU	
EXPECTED	ACTUAL								

GRAIN	AMT.
TOTAL	

HOPS	FORM	AA	IBU	TIME	AMT.
	TOTAL				

WATER TREATMENTS	pH		AMT.

YEAST STRAIN	AMT.

OTHER INGREDIENTS	AMT.

BREWING					
TIME	STEP	[STRIKE, MASH-IN, MASH-OUT, SPARGE, BOIL, KNOCKOUT]	TEMP	VOLUME	GRAVITY
	1.				
	2.				
	3.				
	4.				
	5.				
	6.				

FERMENTATION					
DATE	STEP		START TEMP	END TEMP	GRAVITY	DAYS
	1.				
	2.				
	3.				
	4.				

FERMENTATION ADDITIONS

DATE	ADDITION	AMT.	DAYS

PACKAGING

DATE	FINAL VOLUME	NUMBER OF BOTTLES	NUMBER OF KEGS	READY TO DRINK BY DATE

INGREDIENTS INFORMATION

....

....

....

....

....

....

....

BREWING NOTES

....

....

....

....

....

....

....

TASTING NOTES	ADDITIONAL INFORMATION

UNITS OF MEASUREMENT	
TEMP	
WEIGHT	
VOLUME	

BEER INFO	RATING:	☆ ☆ ☆ ☆ ☆

BEER NAME .... BATCH NO. ....

STYLE .... BATCH VOLUME ....

BREWER .... DATE ....

OG		FG		ABV		SRM		IBU	
EXPECTED	ACTUAL								

GRAIN	AMT.
TOTAL	

HOPS	FORM	AA	IBU	TIME	AMT.
TOTAL					

WATER TREATMENTS	pH		AMT.

YEAST STRAIN	AMT.

OTHER INGREDIENTS	AMT.

BREWING

TIME	STEP	[STRIKE, MASH-IN, MASH-OUT, SPARGE, BOIL, KNOCKOUT]	TEMP	VOLUME	GRAVITY
	1.				
	2.				
	3.				
	4.				
	5.				
	6.				

FERMENTATION

DATE	STEP		START TEMP	END TEMP	GRAVITY	DAYS
	1.					
	2.					
	3.					
	4.					

FERMENTATION ADDITIONS

DATE	ADDITION	AMT.	DAYS

PACKAGING

DATE	FINAL VOLUME	NUMBER OF BOTTLES	NUMBER OF KEGS	READY TO DRINK BY DATE

INGREDIENTS INFORMATION

BREWING NOTES

TASTING NOTES

ADDITIONAL INFORMATION

UNITS OF MEASUREMENT	
TEMP	
WEIGHT	
VOLUME	

BEER INFO

RATING: ☆ ☆ ☆ ☆ ☆

BEER NAME .... BATCH NO. ....

STYLE .... BATCH VOLUME ....

BREWER .... DATE ....

OG		FG		ABV		SRM		IBU	
EXPECTED	ACTUAL								

GRAIN	AMT.
TOTAL	

HOPS	FORM	AA	IBU	TIME	AMT.
TOTAL					

WATER TREATMENTS	pH		AMT.

YEAST STRAIN	AMT.

OTHER INGREDIENTS	AMT.

BREWING

TIME	STEP [STRIKE, MASH-IN, MASH-OUT, SPARGE, BOIL, KNOCKOUT]	TEMP	VOLUME	GRAVITY
	1.			
	2.			
	3.			
	4.			
	5.			
	6.			

FERMENTATION

DATE	STEP	START TEMP	END TEMP	GRAVITY	DAYS
	1.				
	2.				
	3.				
	4.				

FERMENTATION ADDITIONS

DATE	ADDITION	AMT.	DAYS

PACKAGING

DATE	FINAL VOLUME	NUMBER OF BOTTLES	NUMBER OF KEGS	READY TO DRINK BY DATE

INGREDIENTS INFORMATION

....
....
....
....
....
....
....

BREWING NOTES

....
....
....
....
....
....
....

TASTING NOTES

ADDITIONAL INFORMATION

UNITS OF MEASUREMENT	
TEMP	
WEIGHT	
VOLUME	

| BEER INFO | | | | | RATING: | ☆ ☆ ☆ ☆ ☆ |

BEER NAME .... **BATCH NO.** ....

STYLE .... **BATCH VOLUME** ....

BREWER .... **DATE** ....

OG		FG		ABV		SRM		IBU	
EXPECTED	ACTUAL								

GRAIN	AMT.
TOTAL	

HOPS	FORM	AA	IBU	TIME	AMT.
TOTAL					

WATER TREATMENTS	pH		AMT.

YEAST STRAIN	AMT.

OTHER INGREDIENTS	AMT.

BREWING					
TIME	STEP [STRIKE, MASH-IN, MASH-OUT, SPARGE, BOIL, KNOCKOUT]		TEMP	VOLUME	GRAVITY
	1.				
	2.				
	3.				
	4.				
	5.				
	6.				

FERMENTATION					
DATE	STEP	START TEMP	END TEMP	GRAVITY	DAYS
	1.				
	2.				
	3.				
	4.				

FERMENTATION ADDITIONS

DATE	ADDITION	AMT.	DAYS

PACKAGING

DATE	FINAL VOLUME	NUMBER OF BOTTLES	NUMBER OF KEGS	READY TO DRINK BY DATE

INGREDIENTS INFORMATION

....
....
....
....
....
....
....

BREWING NOTES

....
....
....
....
....
....
....

TASTING NOTES

ADDITIONAL INFORMATION

UNITS OF MEASUREMENT	
TEMP	
WEIGHT	
VOLUME	

BEER INFO

RATING: ☆ ☆ ☆ ☆ ☆

BEER NAME .... BATCH NO. ....

STYLE .... BATCH VOLUME ....

BREWER .... DATE ....

OG		FG		ABV		SRM		IBU	
EXPECTED	ACTUAL								

GRAIN	AMT.
TOTAL	

HOPS	FORM	AA	IBU	TIME	AMT.
TOTAL					

WATER TREATMENTS	pH		AMT.

YEAST STRAIN	AMT.

OTHER INGREDIENTS	AMT.

BREWING

TIME	STEP	[STRIKE, MASH-IN, MASH-OUT, SPARGE, BOIL, KNOCKOUT]	TEMP	VOLUME	GRAVITY
	1.				
	2.				
	3.				
	4.				
	5.				
	6.				

FERMENTATION

DATE	STEP	START TEMP	END TEMP	GRAVITY	DAYS
	1.				
	2.				
	3.				
	4.				

FERMENTATION ADDITIONS

DATE	ADDITION	AMT.	DAYS

PACKAGING

DATE	FINAL VOLUME	NUMBER OF BOTTLES	NUMBER OF KEGS	READY TO DRINK BY DATE

INGREDIENTS INFORMATION

....
....
....
....
....
....
....

BREWING NOTES

....
....
....
....
....
....
....

TASTING NOTES

ADDITIONAL INFORMATION

UNITS OF MEASUREMENT	
TEMP	
WEIGHT	
VOLUME	

BEER INFO

RATING: ☆ ☆ ☆ ☆ ☆

BEER NAME .... BATCH NO. ....

STYLE .... BATCH VOLUME ....

BREWER .... DATE ....

OG		FG		ABV		SRM		IBU	
EXPECTED	ACTUAL								

GRAIN	AMT.
TOTAL	

HOPS		FORM	AA	IBU	TIME	AMT.
			TOTAL			

WATER TREATMENTS	pH		AMT.

OTHER INGREDIENTS	AMT.

YEAST STRAIN	AMT.

BREWING

TIME	STEP [STRIKE, MASH-IN, MASH-OUT, SPARGE, BOIL, KNOCKOUT]		TEMP	VOLUME	GRAVITY
	1.				
	2.				
	3.				
	4.				
	5.				
	6.				

FERMENTATION

DATE	STEP		START TEMP	END TEMP	GRAVITY	DAYS
	1.					
	2.					
	3.					
	4.					

FERMENTATION ADDITIONS

DATE	ADDITION	AMT.	DAYS

PACKAGING

DATE	FINAL VOLUME	NUMBER OF BOTTLES	NUMBER OF KEGS	READY TO DRINK BY DATE

INGREDIENTS INFORMATION

....

....

....

....

....

....

....

BREWING NOTES

....

....

....

....

....

....

....

TASTING NOTES

ADDITIONAL INFORMATION

UNITS OF MEASUREMENT	
TEMP	
WEIGHT	
VOLUME	

BEER INFO	RATING: ☆ ☆ ☆ ☆ ☆

BEER NAME .... **BATCH NO.** ....

STYLE .... **BATCH VOLUME** ....

BREWER .... **DATE** ....

OG		FG		ABV		SRM		IBU	
EXPECTED	ACTUAL								

GRAIN	AMT.
TOTAL	

HOPS	FORM	AA	IBU	TIME	AMT.
TOTAL					

WATER TREATMENTS	pH		AMT.

YEAST STRAIN	AMT.

OTHER INGREDIENTS	AMT.

BREWING					
TIME	STEP [STRIKE, MASH-IN, MASH-OUT, SPARGE, BOIL, KNOCKOUT]		TEMP	VOLUME	GRAVITY
	1.				
	2.				
	3.				
	4.				
	5.				
	6.				

FERMENTATION					
DATE	STEP	START TEMP	END TEMP	GRAVITY	DAYS
	1.				
	2.				
	3.				
	4.				

FERMENTATION ADDITIONS

DATE	ADDITION	AMT.	DAYS

PACKAGING

DATE	FINAL VOLUME	NUMBER OF BOTTLES	NUMBER OF KEGS	READY TO DRINK BY DATE

INGREDIENTS INFORMATION

....
....
....
....
....
....
....

BREWING NOTES

....
....
....
....
....
....
....

TASTING NOTES | ADDITIONAL INFORMATION

UNITS OF MEASUREMENT	
TEMP	
WEIGHT	
VOLUME	

BEER INFO	RATING: ☆ ☆ ☆ ☆ ☆

BEER NAME .... BATCH NO. ....

STYLE .... BATCH VOLUME ....

BREWER .... DATE ....

OG		FG		ABV		SRM		IBU	
EXPECTED	ACTUAL								

GRAIN	AMT.
TOTAL	

HOPS		FORM	AA	IBU	TIME	AMT.
		TOTAL				

WATER TREATMENTS	pH		AMT.

OTHER INGREDIENTS	AMT.

YEAST STRAIN	AMT.

BREWING					
TIME	STEP	[STRIKE, MASH-IN, MASH-OUT, SPARGE, BOIL, KNOCKOUT]	TEMP	VOLUME	GRAVITY
	1.				
	2.				
	3.				
	4.				
	5.				
	6.				

FERMENTATION					
DATE	STEP		START TEMP	END TEMP	GRAVITY	DAYS
	1.				
	2.				
	3.				
	4.				

FERMENTATION ADDITIONS

DATE	ADDITION	AMT.	DAYS

PACKAGING

DATE	FINAL VOLUME	NUMBER OF BOTTLES	NUMBER OF KEGS	READY TO DRINK BY DATE

INGREDIENTS INFORMATION

....

....

....

....

....

....

....

BREWING NOTES

....

....

....

....

....

....

....

TASTING NOTES

ADDITIONAL INFORMATION

UNITS OF MEASUREMENT	
TEMP	
WEIGHT	
VOLUME	

BEER INFO

RATING: ☆ ☆ ☆ ☆ ☆

BEER NAME .... BATCH NO. ....

STYLE .... BATCH VOLUME ....

BREWER .... DATE ....

OG		FG		ABV		SRM		IBU	
EXPECTED	ACTUAL								

GRAIN	AMT.
TOTAL	

HOPS	FORM	AA	IBU	TIME	AMT.
TOTAL					

WATER TREATMENTS	pH		AMT.

YEAST STRAIN	AMT.

OTHER INGREDIENTS	AMT.

BREWING

TIME	STEP	[STRIKE, MASH-IN, MASH-OUT, SPARGE, BOIL, KNOCKOUT]	TEMP	VOLUME	GRAVITY
	1.				
	2.				
	3.				
	4.				
	5.				
	6.				

FERMENTATION

DATE	STEP		START TEMP	END TEMP	GRAVITY	DAYS
	1.					
	2.					
	3.					
	4.					

FERMENTATION ADDITIONS

DATE	ADDITION	AMT.	DAYS

PACKAGING

DATE	FINAL VOLUME	NUMBER OF BOTTLES	NUMBER OF KEGS	READY TO DRINK BY DATE

INGREDIENTS INFORMATION

....
....
....
....
....
....
....

BREWING NOTES

....
....
....
....
....
....
....

TASTING NOTES

ADDITIONAL INFORMATION

UNITS OF MEASUREMENT	
TEMP	
WEIGHT	
VOLUME	

BEER INFO						RATING:	☆ ☆ ☆ ☆ ☆

BEER NAME .... BATCH NO. ....

STYLE .... BATCH VOLUME ....

BREWER .... DATE ....

OG		FG		ABV		SRM		IBU	
EXPECTED	ACTUAL								

GRAIN	AMT.
TOTAL	

HOPS	FORM	AA	IBU	TIME	AMT.
		TOTAL			

WATER TREATMENTS	pH		AMT.

YEAST STRAIN	AMT.

OTHER INGREDIENTS	AMT.

BREWING					
TIME	STEP	[STRIKE, MASH-IN, MASH-OUT, SPARGE, BOIL, KNOCKOUT]	TEMP	VOLUME	GRAVITY
	1.				
	2.				
	3.				
	4.				
	5.				
	6.				

FERMENTATION					
DATE	STEP		START TEMP	END TEMP	GRAVITY	DAYS
	1.				
	2.				
	3.				
	4.				

FERMENTATION ADDITIONS

DATE	ADDITION	AMT.	DAYS

PACKAGING

DATE	FINAL VOLUME	NUMBER OF BOTTLES	NUMBER OF KEGS	READY TO DRINK BY DATE

INGREDIENTS INFORMATION

....
....
....
....
....
....
....

BREWING NOTES

....
....
....
....
....
....
....

TASTING NOTES

ADDITIONAL INFORMATION

UNITS OF MEASUREMENT	
TEMP	
WEIGHT	
VOLUME	

BEER INFO

RATING: ☆ ☆ ☆ ☆ ☆

BEER NAME .... BATCH NO. ....

STYLE .... BATCH VOLUME ....

BREWER .... DATE ....

OG		FG		ABV		SRM		IBU	
EXPECTED	ACTUAL								

GRAIN	AMT.
TOTAL	

HOPS	FORM	AA	IBU	TIME	AMT.
TOTAL					

WATER TREATMENTS	pH		AMT.

OTHER INGREDIENTS	AMT.

YEAST STRAIN	AMT.

BREWING

TIME	STEP [STRIKE, MASH-IN, MASH-OUT, SPARGE, BOIL, KNOCKOUT]	TEMP	VOLUME	GRAVITY
	1.			
	2.			
	3.			
	4.			
	5.			
	6.			

FERMENTATION

DATE	STEP	START TEMP	END TEMP	GRAVITY	DAYS
	1.				
	2.				
	3.				
	4.				

FERMENTATION ADDITIONS

DATE	ADDITION	AMT.	DAYS

PACKAGING

DATE	FINAL VOLUME	NUMBER OF BOTTLES	NUMBER OF KEGS	READY TO DRINK BY DATE

INGREDIENTS INFORMATION

....
....
....
....
....
....
....

BREWING NOTES

....
....
....
....
....
....
....

TASTING NOTES	ADDITIONAL INFORMATION

UNITS OF MEASUREMENT	
TEMP	
WEIGHT	
VOLUME	

BEER INFO	RATING: ☆ ☆ ☆ ☆ ☆

BEER NAME .... BATCH NO. ....

STYLE .... BATCH VOLUME ....

BREWER .... DATE ....

OG		FG		ABV		SRM		IBU	
EXPECTED	ACTUAL								

GRAIN	AMT.
TOTAL	

HOPS	FORM	AA	IBU	TIME	AMT.
TOTAL					

WATER TREATMENTS	pH		AMT.

YEAST STRAIN	AMT.

OTHER INGREDIENTS	AMT.

BREWING					
TIME	STEP [STRIKE, MASH-IN, MASH-OUT, SPARGE, BOIL, KNOCKOUT]		TEMP	VOLUME	GRAVITY
	1.				
	2.				
	3.				
	4.				
	5.				
	6.				

FERMENTATION		START TEMP	END TEMP	GRAVITY	DAYS
DATE	STEP				
	1.				
	2.				
	3.				
	4.				

FERMENTATION ADDITIONS

DATE	ADDITION	AMT.	DAYS

PACKAGING

DATE	FINAL VOLUME	NUMBER OF BOTTLES	NUMBER OF KEGS	READY TO DRINK BY DATE

INGREDIENTS INFORMATION

....
....
....
....
....
....
....

BREWING NOTES

....
....
....
....
....
....
....

TASTING NOTES

ADDITIONAL INFORMATION

UNITS OF MEASUREMENT	
TEMP	
WEIGHT	
VOLUME	

| BEER INFO | | | | | | RATING: | ☆ | ☆ | ☆ | ☆ | ☆ |

BEER NAME .... **BATCH NO.** ....

STYLE .... **BATCH VOLUME** ....

BREWER .... **DATE** ....

OG		FG		ABV		SRM		IBU	
EXPECTED	ACTUAL								

GRAIN	AMT.
TOTAL	

HOPS	FORM	AA	IBU	TIME	AMT.
TOTAL					

WATER TREATMENTS	pH		AMT.

OTHER INGREDIENTS	AMT.

YEAST STRAIN	AMT.

BREWING					
TIME	STEP	[STRIKE, MASH-IN, MASH-OUT, SPARGE, BOIL, KNOCKOUT]	TEMP	VOLUME	GRAVITY
	1.				
	2.				
	3.				
	4.				
	5.				
	6.				

FERMENTATION					
DATE	STEP		START TEMP	END TEMP	GRAVITY	DAYS
	1.				
	2.				
	3.				
	4.				

FERMENTATION ADDITIONS

DATE	ADDITION	AMT.	DAYS

PACKAGING

DATE	FINAL VOLUME	NUMBER OF BOTTLES	NUMBER OF KEGS	READY TO DRINK BY DATE

INGREDIENTS INFORMATION

....
....
....
....
....
....
....

BREWING NOTES

....
....
....
....
....
....
....

TASTING NOTES

ADDITIONAL INFORMATION

UNITS OF MEASUREMENT	
TEMP	
WEIGHT	
VOLUME	

| BEER INFO | | | | RATING: | ☆ ☆ ☆ ☆ ☆ |

BEER NAME .... **BATCH NO.** ....

STYLE .... **BATCH VOLUME** ....

BREWER .... **DATE** ....

OG		FG		ABV		SRM		IBU	
EXPECTED	ACTUAL								

GRAIN	AMT.
TOTAL	

HOPS	FORM	AA	IBU	TIME	AMT.
	TOTAL				

WATER TREATMENTS	pH		AMT.

YEAST STRAIN	AMT.

OTHER INGREDIENTS	AMT.

BREWING					
TIME	STEP	[STRIKE, MASH-IN, MASH-OUT, SPARGE, BOIL, KNOCKOUT]	TEMP	VOLUME	GRAVITY
	1.				
	2.				
	3.				
	4.				
	5.				
	6.				

FERMENTATION					
DATE	STEP		START TEMP	END TEMP	GRAVITY	DAYS
	1.				
	2.				
	3.				
	4.				

FERMENTATION ADDITIONS

DATE	ADDITION	AMT.	DAYS

PACKAGING

DATE	FINAL VOLUME	NUMBER OF BOTTLES	NUMBER OF KEGS	READY TO DRINK BY DATE

INGREDIENTS INFORMATION

....
....
....
....
....
....
....

BREWING NOTES

....
....
....
....
....
....
....

TASTING NOTES	ADDITIONAL INFORMATION

UNITS OF MEASUREMENT

TEMP	
WEIGHT	
VOLUME	

BEER INFO

RATING: ☆ ☆ ☆ ☆ ☆

BEER NAME .... BATCH NO. ....

STYLE .... BATCH VOLUME ....

BREWER .... DATE ....

OG		FG		ABV		SRM		IBU	
EXPECTED	ACTUAL								

GRAIN	AMT.
TOTAL	

HOPS	FORM	AA	IBU	TIME	AMT.
TOTAL					

WATER TREATMENTS	pH		AMT.

YEAST STRAIN	AMT.

OTHER INGREDIENTS	AMT.

BREWING

TIME	STEP	[STRIKE, MASH-IN, MASH-OUT, SPARGE, BOIL, KNOCKOUT]	TEMP	VOLUME	GRAVITY
	1.				
	2.				
	3.				
	4.				
	5.				
	6.				

FERMENTATION

DATE	STEP		START TEMP	END TEMP	GRAVITY	DAYS
	1.					
	2.					
	3.					
	4.					

FERMENTATION ADDITIONS

DATE	ADDITION	AMT.	DAYS

PACKAGING

DATE	FINAL VOLUME	NUMBER OF BOTTLES	NUMBER OF KEGS	READY TO DRINK BY DATE

INGREDIENTS INFORMATION

....

....

....

....

....

....

....

BREWING NOTES

....

....

....

....

....

....

....

TASTING NOTES	ADDITIONAL INFORMATION

UNITS OF MEASUREMENT	
TEMP	
WEIGHT	
VOLUME	

BEER INFO			RATING:	☆ ☆ ☆ ☆ ☆

BEER NAME .... BATCH NO. ....

STYLE .... BATCH VOLUME ....

BREWER .... DATE ....

OG		FG		ABV		SRM		IBU	
EXPECTED	ACTUAL								

GRAIN	AMT.
TOTAL	

HOPS	FORM	AA	IBU	TIME	AMT.
TOTAL					

WATER TREATMENTS	pH		AMT.

YEAST STRAIN	AMT.

OTHER INGREDIENTS	AMT.

BREWING					
TIME	STEP	[STRIKE, MASH-IN, MASH-OUT, SPARGE, BOIL, KNOCKOUT]	TEMP	VOLUME	GRAVITY
	1.				
	2.				
	3.				
	4.				
	5.				
	6.				

FERMENTATION					
DATE	STEP		START TEMP	END TEMP	GRAVITY	DAYS
	1.					
	2.					
	3.					
	4.					

FERMENTATION ADDITIONS

DATE	ADDITION	AMT.	DAYS

PACKAGING

DATE	FINAL VOLUME	NUMBER OF BOTTLES	NUMBER OF KEGS	READY TO DRINK BY DATE

INGREDIENTS INFORMATION

....
....
....
....
....
....
....

BREWING NOTES

....
....
....
....
....
....
....

TASTING NOTES

ADDITIONAL INFORMATION

UNITS OF MEASUREMENT	
TEMP	
WEIGHT	
VOLUME	

BEER INFO

RATING: ☆ ☆ ☆ ☆ ☆

BEER NAME .... BATCH NO. ....

STYLE .... BATCH VOLUME ....

BREWER .... DATE ....

OG		FG		ABV		SRM		IBU	
EXPECTED	ACTUAL								

GRAIN	AMT.
TOTAL	

HOPS	FORM	AA	IBU	TIME	AMT.
TOTAL					

WATER TREATMENTS	pH		AMT.

YEAST STRAIN	AMT.

OTHER INGREDIENTS	AMT.

BREWING

TIME	STEP [STRIKE, MASH-IN, MASH-OUT, SPARGE, BOIL, KNOCKOUT]	TEMP	VOLUME	GRAVITY
	1.			
	2.			
	3.			
	4.			
	5.			
	6.			

FERMENTATION

DATE	STEP	START TEMP	END TEMP	GRAVITY	DAYS
	1.				
	2.				
	3.				
	4.				

FERMENTATION ADDITIONS

DATE	ADDITION	AMT.	DAYS

PACKAGING

DATE	FINAL VOLUME	NUMBER OF BOTTLES	NUMBER OF KEGS	READY TO DRINK BY DATE

INGREDIENTS INFORMATION

....
....
....
....
....
....
....

BREWING NOTES

....
....
....
....
....
....
....

TASTING NOTES

ADDITIONAL INFORMATION

UNITS OF MEASUREMENT	
TEMP	
WEIGHT	
VOLUME	

BEER INFO

RATING: ☆ ☆ ☆ ☆ ☆

BEER NAME .... BATCH NO. ....

STYLE .... BATCH VOLUME ....

BREWER .... DATE ....

OG		FG		ABV		SRM		IBU	
EXPECTED	ACTUAL								

GRAIN	AMT.
TOTAL	

HOPS	FORM	AA	IBU	TIME	AMT.
TOTAL					

WATER TREATMENTS	pH		AMT.

OTHER INGREDIENTS	AMT.

YEAST STRAIN	AMT.

BREWING

TIME	STEP	[STRIKE, MASH-IN, MASH-OUT, SPARGE, BOIL, KNOCKOUT]	TEMP	VOLUME	GRAVITY
	1.				
	2.				
	3.				
	4.				
	5.				
	6.				

FERMENTATION

DATE	STEP	START TEMP	END TEMP	GRAVITY	DAYS
	1.				
	2.				
	3.				
	4.				

FERMENTATION ADDITIONS

DATE	ADDITION	AMT.	DAYS

PACKAGING

DATE	FINAL VOLUME	NUMBER OF BOTTLES	NUMBER OF KEGS	READY TO DRINK BY DATE

INGREDIENTS INFORMATION

....
....
....
....
....
....
....

BREWING NOTES

....
....
....
....
....
....
....

TASTING NOTES

ADDITIONAL INFORMATION

UNITS OF MEASUREMENT	
TEMP	
WEIGHT	
VOLUME	

BEER INFO

RATING: ☆ ☆ ☆ ☆ ☆

BEER NAME .... BATCH NO. ....

STYLE .... BATCH VOLUME ....

BREWER .... DATE ....

OG		FG		ABV		SRM		IBU	
EXPECTED	ACTUAL								

GRAIN	AMT.
TOTAL	

HOPS	FORM	AA	IBU	TIME	AMT.
TOTAL					

WATER TREATMENTS	pH		AMT.

YEAST STRAIN	AMT.

OTHER INGREDIENTS	AMT.

BREWING

TIME	STEP	[STRIKE, MASH-IN, MASH-OUT, SPARGE, BOIL, KNOCKOUT]	TEMP	VOLUME	GRAVITY
	1.				
	2.				
	3.				
	4.				
	5.				
	6.				

FERMENTATION

DATE	STEP	START TEMP	END TEMP	GRAVITY	DAYS
	1.				
	2.				
	3.				
	4.				

FERMENTATION ADDITIONS

DATE	ADDITION	AMT.	DAYS

PACKAGING

DATE	FINAL VOLUME	NUMBER OF BOTTLES	NUMBER OF KEGS	READY TO DRINK BY DATE

INGREDIENTS INFORMATION

....
....
....
....
....
....
....

BREWING NOTES

....
....
....
....
....
....
....

TASTING NOTES

ADDITIONAL INFORMATION

UNITS OF MEASUREMENT	
TEMP	
WEIGHT	
VOLUME	

BEER INFO	RATING: ☆ ☆ ☆ ☆ ☆

BEER NAME .... BATCH NO. ....

STYLE .... BATCH VOLUME ....

BREWER .... DATE ....

OG		FG		ABV		SRM		IBU	
EXPECTED	ACTUAL								

GRAIN	AMT.
TOTAL	

HOPS	FORM	AA	IBU	TIME	AMT.
TOTAL					

WATER TREATMENTS	pH		AMT.

YEAST STRAIN	AMT.

OTHER INGREDIENTS	AMT.

BREWING					
TIME	STEP	[STRIKE, MASH-IN, MASH-OUT, SPARGE, BOIL, KNOCKOUT]	TEMP	VOLUME	GRAVITY
	1.				
	2.				
	3.				
	4.				
	5.				
	6.				

FERMENTATION					
DATE	STEP		START TEMP	END TEMP	GRAVITY	DAYS
	1.				
	2.				
	3.				
	4.				

FERMENTATION ADDITIONS

DATE	ADDITION	AMT.	DAYS

PACKAGING

DATE	FINAL VOLUME	NUMBER OF BOTTLES	NUMBER OF KEGS	READY TO DRINK BY DATE

INGREDIENTS INFORMATION

BREWING NOTES

TASTING NOTES

ADDITIONAL INFORMATION

UNITS OF MEASUREMENT	
TEMP	
WEIGHT	
VOLUME	

BEER INFO		RATING: ☆ ☆ ☆ ☆ ☆

BEER NAME .... BATCH NO. ....

STYLE .... BATCH VOLUME ....

BREWER .... DATE ....

OG		FG		ABV		SRM		IBU	
EXPECTED	ACTUAL								

GRAIN	AMT.
TOTAL	

HOPS	FORM	AA	IBU	TIME	AMT.
TOTAL					

WATER TREATMENTS	pH		AMT.

YEAST STRAIN	AMT.

OTHER INGREDIENTS	AMT.

BREWING					
TIME	STEP	[STRIKE, MASH-IN, MASH-OUT, SPARGE, BOIL, KNOCKOUT]	TEMP	VOLUME	GRAVITY
	1.				
	2.				
	3.				
	4.				
	5.				
	6.				

FERMENTATION					
DATE	STEP		START TEMP	END TEMP	GRAVITY	DAYS
	1.				
	2.				
	3.				
	4.				

FERMENTATION ADDITIONS

DATE	ADDITION	AMT.	DAYS

PACKAGING

DATE	FINAL VOLUME	NUMBER OF BOTTLES	NUMBER OF KEGS	READY TO DRINK BY DATE

INGREDIENTS INFORMATION

....
....
....
....
....
....
....

BREWING NOTES

....
....
....
....
....
....
....

TASTING NOTES

ADDITIONAL INFORMATION

UNITS OF MEASUREMENT	
TEMP	
WEIGHT	
VOLUME	

BEER INFO

RATING: ☆ ☆ ☆ ☆ ☆

BEER NAME .... BATCH NO. ....

STYLE .... BATCH VOLUME ....

BREWER .... DATE ....

OG		FG		ABV		SRM		IBU	
EXPECTED	ACTUAL								

GRAIN	AMT.
TOTAL	

HOPS		FORM	AA	IBU	TIME	AMT.
				TOTAL		

WATER TREATMENTS	pH		AMT.

OTHER INGREDIENTS	AMT.

YEAST STRAIN	AMT.

BREWING

TIME	STEP	[STRIKE, MASH-IN, MASH-OUT, SPARGE, BOIL, KNOCKOUT]	TEMP	VOLUME	GRAVITY
	1.				
	2.				
	3.				
	4.				
	5.				
	6.				

FERMENTATION

DATE	STEP	START TEMP	END TEMP	GRAVITY	DAYS
	1.				
	2.				
	3.				
	4.				

FERMENTATION ADDITIONS

DATE	ADDITION	AMT.	DAYS

PACKAGING

DATE	FINAL VOLUME	NUMBER OF BOTTLES	NUMBER OF KEGS	READY TO DRINK BY DATE

INGREDIENTS INFORMATION

....
....
....
....
....
....
....

BREWING NOTES

....
....
....
....
....
....
....

TASTING NOTES

ADDITIONAL INFORMATION

UNITS OF MEASUREMENT	
TEMP	
WEIGHT	
VOLUME	

BEER INFO	RATING:	☆ ☆ ☆ ☆ ☆

BEER NAME .... BATCH NO. ....

STYLE .... BATCH VOLUME ....

BREWER .... DATE ....

OG		FG		ABV		SRM		IBU	
EXPECTED	ACTUAL								

GRAIN	AMT.
TOTAL	

HOPS	FORM	AA	IBU	TIME	AMT.
TOTAL					

WATER TREATMENTS	pH		AMT.

YEAST STRAIN	AMT.

OTHER INGREDIENTS	AMT.

BREWING					
TIME	STEP [STRIKE, MASH-IN, MASH-OUT, SPARGE, BOIL, KNOCKOUT]		TEMP	VOLUME	GRAVITY
	1.				
	2.				
	3.				
	4.				
	5.				
	6.				

FERMENTATION					
DATE	STEP	START TEMP	END TEMP	GRAVITY	DAYS
	1.				
	2.				
	3.				
	4.				

FERMENTATION ADDITIONS

DATE	ADDITION	AMT.	DAYS

PACKAGING

DATE	FINAL VOLUME	NUMBER OF BOTTLES	NUMBER OF KEGS	READY TO DRINK BY DATE

INGREDIENTS INFORMATION

BREWING NOTES

TASTING NOTES

ADDITIONAL INFORMATION

UNITS OF MEASUREMENT	
TEMP	
WEIGHT	
VOLUME	

BEER INFO					RATING:	☆ ☆ ☆ ☆ ☆

BEER NAME .... BATCH NO. ....

STYLE .... BATCH VOLUME ....

BREWER .... DATE ....

OG		FG		ABV		SRM		IBU	
EXPECTED	ACTUAL								

GRAIN	AMT.
TOTAL	

HOPS	FORM	AA	IBU	TIME	AMT.
				TOTAL	

WATER TREATMENTS	pH		AMT.

YEAST STRAIN	AMT.

OTHER INGREDIENTS	AMT.

BREWING					
TIME	STEP	[STRIKE, MASH-IN, MASH-OUT, SPARGE, BOIL, KNOCKOUT]	TEMP	VOLUME	GRAVITY
	1.				
	2.				
	3.				
	4.				
	5.				
	6.				

FERMENTATION					
DATE	STEP		START TEMP	END TEMP	GRAVITY	DAYS
	1.					
	2.					
	3.					
	4.					

FERMENTATION ADDITIONS

DATE	ADDITION	AMT.	DAYS

PACKAGING

DATE	FINAL VOLUME	NUMBER OF BOTTLES	NUMBER OF KEGS	READY TO DRINK BY DATE

INGREDIENTS INFORMATION

BREWING NOTES

TASTING NOTES | ADDITIONAL INFORMATION

UNITS OF MEASUREMENT	
TEMP	
WEIGHT	
VOLUME	

BEER INFO		RATING: ☆ ☆ ☆ ☆ ☆

BEER NAME .... BATCH NO. ....

STYLE .... BATCH VOLUME ....

BREWER .... DATE ....

OG		FG	ABV	SRM	IBU
EXPECTED	ACTUAL				

GRAIN	AMT.
TOTAL	

HOPS	FORM	AA	IBU	TIME	AMT.
TOTAL					

WATER TREATMENTS	pH		AMT.

YEAST STRAIN	AMT.

OTHER INGREDIENTS	AMT.

BREWING

TIME	STEP [STRIKE, MASH-IN, MASH-OUT, SPARGE, BOIL, KNOCKOUT]	TEMP	VOLUME	GRAVITY
	1.			
	2.			
	3.			
	4.			
	5.			
	6.			

FERMENTATION

DATE	STEP	START TEMP	END TEMP	GRAVITY	DAYS
	1.				
	2.				
	3.				
	4.				

FERMENTATION ADDITIONS

DATE	ADDITION	AMT.	DAYS

PACKAGING

DATE	FINAL VOLUME	NUMBER OF BOTTLES	NUMBER OF KEGS	READY TO DRINK BY DATE

INGREDIENTS INFORMATION

....
....
....
....
....
....
....

BREWING NOTES

....
....
....
....
....
....
....

TASTING NOTES | ADDITIONAL INFORMATION

UNITS OF MEASUREMENT	
TEMP	
WEIGHT	
VOLUME	

BEER INFO	RATING:	☆ ☆ ☆ ☆ ☆

BEER NAME .... BATCH NO. ....

STYLE .... BATCH VOLUME ....

BREWER .... DATE ....

OG		FG		ABV		SRM		IBU	
EXPECTED	ACTUAL								

GRAIN	AMT.
TOTAL	

HOPS	FORM	AA	IBU	TIME	AMT.
TOTAL					

WATER TREATMENTS	pH		AMT.

OTHER INGREDIENTS	AMT.

YEAST STRAIN	AMT.

BREWING						
TIME	STEP	[STRIKE, MASH-IN, MASH-OUT, SPARGE, BOIL, KNOCKOUT]		TEMP	VOLUME	GRAVITY
	1.					
	2.					
	3.					
	4.					
	5.					
	6.					

FERMENTATION					
DATE	STEP	START TEMP	END TEMP	GRAVITY	DAYS
	1.				
	2.				
	3.				
	4.				

FERMENTATION ADDITIONS			
DATE	ADDITION	AMT.	DAYS

PACKAGING				
DATE	FINAL VOLUME	NUMBER OF BOTTLES	NUMBER OF KEGS	READY TO DRINK BY DATE

INGREDIENTS INFORMATION

....
....
....
....
....
....
....

BREWING NOTES

....
....
....
....
....
....
....

TASTING NOTES	ADDITIONAL INFORMATION

UNITS OF MEASUREMENT	
TEMP	
WEIGHT	
VOLUME	

BEER INFO

RATING: ☆ ☆ ☆ ☆ ☆

BEER NAME .... BATCH NO. ....

STYLE .... BATCH VOLUME ....

BREWER .... DATE ....

OG		FG		ABV		SRM		IBU	
EXPECTED	ACTUAL								

GRAIN	AMT.
TOTAL	

HOPS		FORM	AA	IBU	TIME	AMT.
	TOTAL					

WATER TREATMENTS	pH		AMT.

OTHER INGREDIENTS	AMT.

YEAST STRAIN	AMT.

BREWING

TIME	STEP [STRIKE, MASH-IN, MASH-OUT, SPARGE, BOIL, KNOCKOUT]	TEMP	VOLUME	GRAVITY
	1.			
	2.			
	3.			
	4.			
	5.			
	6.			

FERMENTATION

DATE	STEP	START TEMP	END TEMP	GRAVITY	DAYS
	1.				
	2.				
	3.				
	4.				

FERMENTATION ADDITIONS

DATE	ADDITION	AMT.	DAYS

PACKAGING

DATE	FINAL VOLUME	NUMBER OF BOTTLES	NUMBER OF KEGS	READY TO DRINK BY DATE

INGREDIENTS INFORMATION

....
....
....
....
....
....
....

BREWING NOTES

....
....
....
....
....
....
....

TASTING NOTES	ADDITIONAL INFORMATION

UNITS OF MEASUREMENT	
TEMP	
WEIGHT	
VOLUME	

BEER INFO

RATING: ☆ ☆ ☆ ☆ ☆

BEER NAME .... BATCH NO. ....

STYLE .... BATCH VOLUME ....

BREWER .... DATE ....

OG		FG		ABV		SRM		IBU	
EXPECTED	ACTUAL								

GRAIN	AMT.
TOTAL	

HOPS	FORM	AA	IBU	TIME	AMT.
TOTAL					

WATER TREATMENTS	pH		AMT.

YEAST STRAIN	AMT.

OTHER INGREDIENTS	AMT.

BREWING

TIME	STEP [STRIKE, MASH-IN, MASH-OUT, SPARGE, BOIL, KNOCKOUT]	TEMP	VOLUME	GRAVITY
	1.			
	2.			
	3.			
	4.			
	5.			
	6.			

FERMENTATION

DATE	STEP	START TEMP	END TEMP	GRAVITY	DAYS
	1.				
	2.				
	3.				
	4.				

FERMENTATION ADDITIONS

DATE	ADDITION	AMT.	DAYS

PACKAGING

DATE	FINAL VOLUME	NUMBER OF BOTTLES	NUMBER OF KEGS	READY TO DRINK BY DATE

INGREDIENTS INFORMATION

....
....
....
....
....
....
....

BREWING NOTES

....
....
....
....
....
....
....

TASTING NOTES

ADDITIONAL INFORMATION

UNITS OF MEASUREMENT	
TEMP	
WEIGHT	
VOLUME	

BEER INFO

RATING: ☆ ☆ ☆ ☆ ☆

BEER NAME .... BATCH NO. ....

STYLE .... BATCH VOLUME ....

BREWER .... DATE ....

OG		FG		ABV		SRM		IBU	
EXPECTED	ACTUAL								

GRAIN	AMT.
TOTAL	

HOPS		FORM	AA	IBU	TIME	AMT.
			TOTAL			

WATER TREATMENTS	pH		AMT.

YEAST STRAIN	AMT.

OTHER INGREDIENTS	AMT.

BREWING

TIME	STEP	[STRIKE, MASH-IN, MASH-OUT, SPARGE, BOIL, KNOCKOUT]	TEMP	VOLUME	GRAVITY
	1.				
	2.				
	3.				
	4.				
	5.				
	6.				

FERMENTATION

DATE	STEP	START TEMP	END TEMP	GRAVITY	DAYS
	1.				
	2.				
	3.				
	4.				

FERMENTATION ADDITIONS			
DATE	ADDITION	AMT.	DAYS

PACKAGING				
DATE	FINAL VOLUME	NUMBER OF BOTTLES	NUMBER OF KEGS	READY TO DRINK BY DATE

INGREDIENTS INFORMATION

....
....
....
....
....
....
....

BREWING NOTES

....
....
....
....
....
....
....

TASTING NOTES

ADDITIONAL INFORMATION

UNITS OF MEASUREMENT	
TEMP	
WEIGHT	
VOLUME	

BEER INFO	RATING: ☆ ☆ ☆ ☆ ☆

BEER NAME .... **BATCH NO.** ....

STYLE .... **BATCH VOLUME** ....

BREWER .... **DATE** ....

OG		FG		ABV		SRM		IBU	
EXPECTED	ACTUAL								

GRAIN	AMT.
TOTAL	

HOPS	FORM	AA	IBU	TIME	AMT.
TOTAL					

WATER TREATMENTS	pH		AMT.

YEAST STRAIN	AMT.

OTHER INGREDIENTS	AMT.

BREWING

TIME	STEP [STRIKE, MASH-IN, MASH-OUT, SPARGE, BOIL, KNOCKOUT]	TEMP	VOLUME	GRAVITY
	1.			
	2.			
	3.			
	4.			
	5.			
	6.			

FERMENTATION

DATE	STEP	START TEMP	END TEMP	GRAVITY	DAYS
	1.				
	2.				
	3.				
	4.				

FERMENTATION ADDITIONS

DATE	ADDITION	AMT.	DAYS

PACKAGING

DATE	FINAL VOLUME	NUMBER OF BOTTLES	NUMBER OF KEGS	READY TO DRINK BY DATE

INGREDIENTS INFORMATION

....
....
....
....
....
....
....

BREWING NOTES

....
....
....
....
....
....
....

TASTING NOTES

ADDITIONAL INFORMATION

UNITS OF MEASUREMENT	
TEMP	
WEIGHT	
VOLUME	

BEER INFO

RATING: ☆ ☆ ☆ ☆ ☆

BEER NAME .... BATCH NO. ....

STYLE .... BATCH VOLUME ....

BREWER .... DATE ....

OG		FG		ABV		SRM		IBU	
EXPECTED	ACTUAL								

GRAIN	AMT.
TOTAL	

HOPS	FORM	AA	IBU	TIME	AMT.
TOTAL					

WATER TREATMENTS	pH		AMT.

YEAST STRAIN	AMT.

OTHER INGREDIENTS	AMT.

BREWING

TIME	STEP	[STRIKE, MASH-IN, MASH-OUT, SPARGE, BOIL, KNOCKOUT]	TEMP	VOLUME	GRAVITY
	1.				
	2.				
	3.				
	4.				
	5.				
	6.				

FERMENTATION

DATE	STEP		START TEMP	END TEMP	GRAVITY	DAYS
	1.					
	2.					
	3.					
	4.					

FERMENTATION ADDITIONS

DATE	ADDITION	AMT.	DAYS

PACKAGING

DATE	FINAL VOLUME	NUMBER OF BOTTLES	NUMBER OF KEGS	READY TO DRINK BY DATE

INGREDIENTS INFORMATION

....

....

....

....

....

....

....

BREWING NOTES

....

....

....

....

....

....

....

TASTING NOTES

ADDITIONAL INFORMATION

UNITS OF MEASUREMENT	
TEMP	
WEIGHT	
VOLUME	

| BEER INFO | | | | RATING: | ☆ ☆ ☆ ☆ ☆ |

BEER NAME .... **BATCH NO.** ....

STYLE .... **BATCH VOLUME** ....

BREWER .... **DATE** ....

OG		FG		ABV		SRM		IBU	
EXPECTED	ACTUAL								

GRAIN		AMT.
	TOTAL	

HOPS	FORM	AA	IBU	TIME	AMT.
			TOTAL		

WATER TREATMENTS	pH		AMT.

YEAST STRAIN	AMT.

OTHER INGREDIENTS	AMT.

BREWING

TIME	STEP [STRIKE, MASH-IN, MASH-OUT, SPARGE, BOIL, KNOCKOUT]	TEMP	VOLUME	GRAVITY
	1.			
	2.			
	3.			
	4.			
	5.			
	6.			

FERMENTATION

DATE	STEP	START TEMP	END TEMP	GRAVITY	DAYS
	1.				
	2.				
	3.				
	4.				

FERMENTATION ADDITIONS

DATE	ADDITION	AMT.	DAYS

PACKAGING

DATE	FINAL VOLUME	NUMBER OF BOTTLES	NUMBER OF KEGS	READY TO DRINK BY DATE

INGREDIENTS INFORMATION

....
....
....
....
....
....
....

BREWING NOTES

....
....
....
....
....
....
....

TASTING NOTES

ADDITIONAL INFORMATION

UNITS OF MEASUREMENT	
TEMP	
WEIGHT	
VOLUME	

BEER INFO

RATING: ☆ ☆ ☆ ☆ ☆

BEER NAME .... BATCH NO. ....

STYLE .... BATCH VOLUME ....

BREWER .... DATE ....

OG		FG		ABV		SRM		IBU	
EXPECTED	ACTUAL								

GRAIN	AMT.
TOTAL	

HOPS	FORM	AA	IBU	TIME	AMT.
TOTAL					

WATER TREATMENTS	pH		AMT.

YEAST STRAIN	AMT.

OTHER INGREDIENTS	AMT.

BREWING

TIME	STEP	[STRIKE, MASH-IN, MASH-OUT, SPARGE, BOIL, KNOCKOUT]	TEMP	VOLUME	GRAVITY
	1.				
	2.				
	3.				
	4.				
	5.				
	6.				

FERMENTATION

DATE	STEP		START TEMP	END TEMP	GRAVITY	DAYS
	1.					
	2.					
	3.					
	4.					

FERMENTATION ADDITIONS

DATE	ADDITION	AMT.	DAYS

PACKAGING

DATE	FINAL VOLUME	NUMBER OF BOTTLES	NUMBER OF KEGS	READY TO DRINK BY DATE

INGREDIENTS INFORMATION

....
....
....
....
....
....
....

BREWING NOTES

....
....
....
....
....
....
....

TASTING NOTES

ADDITIONAL INFORMATION

UNITS OF MEASUREMENT	
TEMP	
WEIGHT	
VOLUME	

BEER INFO	RATING: ☆ ☆ ☆ ☆ ☆

BEER NAME .... BATCH NO. ....

STYLE .... BATCH VOLUME ....

BREWER .... DATE ....

OG		FG		ABV		SRM		IBU	
EXPECTED	ACTUAL								

GRAIN	AMT.
TOTAL	

HOPS		FORM	AA	IBU	TIME	AMT.
		TOTAL				

WATER TREATMENTS	pH		AMT.

YEAST STRAIN	AMT.

OTHER INGREDIENTS	AMT.

BREWING					
TIME	STEP	[STRIKE, MASH-IN, MASH-OUT, SPARGE, BOIL, KNOCKOUT]	TEMP	VOLUME	GRAVITY
	1.				
	2.				
	3.				
	4.				
	5.				
	6.				

FERMENTATION					
DATE	STEP	START TEMP	END TEMP	GRAVITY	DAYS
	1.				
	2.				
	3.				
	4.				

FERMENTATION ADDITIONS

DATE	ADDITION	AMT.	DAYS

PACKAGING

DATE	FINAL VOLUME	NUMBER OF BOTTLES	NUMBER OF KEGS	READY TO DRINK BY DATE

INGREDIENTS INFORMATION

....
....
....
....
....
....
....

BREWING NOTES

....
....
....
....
....
....
....

TASTING NOTES

ADDITIONAL INFORMATION

UNITS OF MEASUREMENT	
TEMP	
WEIGHT	
VOLUME	

BEER INFO

RATING: ☆ ☆ ☆ ☆ ☆

BEER NAME .... BATCH NO. ....

STYLE .... BATCH VOLUME ....

BREWER .... DATE ....

OG		FG		ABV		SRM		IBU	
EXPECTED	ACTUAL								

GRAIN	AMT.
TOTAL	

HOPS		FORM	AA	IBU	TIME	AMT.
		TOTAL				

WATER TREATMENTS	pH		AMT.

YEAST STRAIN	AMT.

OTHER INGREDIENTS	AMT.

BREWING

TIME	STEP [STRIKE, MASH-IN, MASH-OUT, SPARGE, BOIL, KNOCKOUT]	TEMP	VOLUME	GRAVITY
	1.			
	2.			
	3.			
	4.			
	5.			
	6.			

FERMENTATION

DATE	STEP	START TEMP	END TEMP	GRAVITY	DAYS
	1.				
	2.				
	3.				
	4.				

FERMENTATION ADDITIONS

DATE	ADDITION	AMT.	DAYS

PACKAGING

DATE	FINAL VOLUME	NUMBER OF BOTTLES	NUMBER OF KEGS	READY TO DRINK BY DATE

INGREDIENTS INFORMATION

BREWING NOTES

TASTING NOTES

ADDITIONAL INFORMATION

UNITS OF MEASUREMENT	
TEMP	
WEIGHT	
VOLUME	

BEER INFO			RATING:	☆ ☆ ☆ ☆ ☆

BEER NAME .... BATCH NO. ....

STYLE .... BATCH VOLUME ....

BREWER .... DATE ....

OG		FG		ABV		SRM		IBU	
EXPECTED	ACTUAL								

GRAIN	AMT.
TOTAL	

HOPS	FORM	AA	IBU	TIME	AMT.
TOTAL					

WATER TREATMENTS	pH		AMT.

OTHER INGREDIENTS	AMT.

YEAST STRAIN	AMT.

BREWING

TIME	STEP	[STRIKE, MASH-IN, MASH-OUT, SPARGE, BOIL, KNOCKOUT]	TEMP	VOLUME	GRAVITY
	1.				
	2.				
	3.				
	4.				
	5.				
	6.				

FERMENTATION

DATE	STEP	START TEMP	END TEMP	GRAVITY	DAYS
	1.				
	2.				
	3.				
	4.				

FERMENTATION ADDITIONS

DATE	ADDITION	AMT.	DAYS

PACKAGING

DATE	FINAL VOLUME	NUMBER OF BOTTLES	NUMBER OF KEGS	READY TO DRINK BY DATE

INGREDIENTS INFORMATION

....

....

....

....

....

....

....

BREWING NOTES

....

....

....

....

....

....

....

TASTING NOTES

ADDITIONAL INFORMATION

UNITS OF MEASUREMENT	
TEMP	
WEIGHT	
VOLUME	

BEER INFO	RATING: ☆ ☆ ☆ ☆ ☆

BEER NAME .... **BATCH NO.** ....

STYLE .... **BATCH VOLUME** ....

BREWER .... **DATE** ....

OG		FG		ABV		SRM		IBU	
EXPECTED	ACTUAL								

GRAIN	AMT.
TOTAL	

HOPS	FORM	AA	IBU	TIME	AMT.
TOTAL					

WATER TREATMENTS	pH		AMT.

OTHER INGREDIENTS	AMT.

YEAST STRAIN	AMT.

BREWING					
TIME	STEP [STRIKE, MASH-IN, MASH-OUT, SPARGE, BOIL, KNOCKOUT]		TEMP	VOLUME	GRAVITY
	1.				
	2.				
	3.				
	4.				
	5.				
	6.				

FERMENTATION					
DATE	STEP	START TEMP	END TEMP	GRAVITY	DAYS
	1.				
	2.				
	3.				
	4.				

FERMENTATION ADDITIONS

DATE	ADDITION	AMT.	DAYS

PACKAGING

DATE	FINAL VOLUME	NUMBER OF BOTTLES	NUMBER OF KEGS	READY TO DRINK BY DATE

INGREDIENTS INFORMATION

BREWING NOTES

TASTING NOTES

ADDITIONAL INFORMATION

UNITS OF MEASUREMENT	
TEMP	
WEIGHT	
VOLUME	

| BEER INFO | | | | RATING: | ☆ ☆ ☆ ☆ ☆ |

BEER NAME .... **BATCH NO.** ....

STYLE .... **BATCH VOLUME** ....

BREWER .... **DATE** ....

OG		FG		ABV		SRM		IBU	
EXPECTED	ACTUAL								

GRAIN	AMT.
TOTAL	

HOPS		FORM	AA	IBU	TIME	AMT.
			TOTAL		

WATER TREATMENTS	pH		AMT.

YEAST STRAIN	AMT.

OTHER INGREDIENTS	AMT.

BREWING					
TIME	STEP	[STRIKE, MASH-IN, MASH-OUT, SPARGE, BOIL, KNOCKOUT]	TEMP	VOLUME	GRAVITY
	1.				
	2.				
	3.				
	4.				
	5.				
	6.				

FERMENTATION					
DATE	STEP		START TEMP	END TEMP	GRAVITY	DAYS
	1.					
	2.					
	3.					
	4.					

FERMENTATION ADDITIONS

DATE	ADDITION	AMT.	DAYS

PACKAGING

DATE	FINAL VOLUME	NUMBER OF BOTTLES	NUMBER OF KEGS	READY TO DRINK BY DATE

INGREDIENTS INFORMATION

....
....
....
....
....
....
....

BREWING NOTES

....
....
....
....
....
....
....

TASTING NOTES

ADDITIONAL INFORMATION

UNITS OF MEASUREMENT	
TEMP	
WEIGHT	
VOLUME	

BEER INFO	RATING: ☆ ☆ ☆ ☆ ☆

BEER NAME .... BATCH NO. ....

STYLE .... BATCH VOLUME ....

BREWER .... DATE ....

OG		FG		ABV		SRM		IBU	
EXPECTED	ACTUAL								

GRAIN	AMT.
TOTAL	

HOPS	FORM	AA	IBU	TIME	AMT.
TOTAL					

WATER TREATMENTS	pH		AMT.

YEAST STRAIN	AMT.

OTHER INGREDIENTS	AMT.

BREWING					
TIME	STEP	[STRIKE, MASH-IN, MASH-OUT, SPARGE, BOIL, KNOCKOUT]	TEMP	VOLUME	GRAVITY
	1.				
	2.				
	3.				
	4.				
	5.				
	6.				

FERMENTATION					
DATE	STEP		START TEMP	END TEMP	GRAVITY	DAYS
	1.				
	2.				
	3.				
	4.				

FERMENTATION ADDITIONS

DATE	ADDITION	AMT.	DAYS

PACKAGING

DATE	FINAL VOLUME	NUMBER OF BOTTLES	NUMBER OF KEGS	READY TO DRINK BY DATE

INGREDIENTS INFORMATION

....
....
....
....
....
....
....

BREWING NOTES

....
....
....
....
....
....
....

TASTING NOTES

ADDITIONAL INFORMATION

UNITS OF MEASUREMENT	
TEMP	
WEIGHT	
VOLUME	

BEER INFO				RATING: ☆ ☆ ☆ ☆ ☆

BEER NAME .... BATCH NO. ....

STYLE .... BATCH VOLUME ....

BREWER .... DATE ....

OG		FG		ABV		SRM		IBU	
EXPECTED	ACTUAL								

GRAIN	AMT.
TOTAL	

HOPS	FORM	AA	IBU	TIME	AMT.
TOTAL					

WATER TREATMENTS	pH		AMT.

YEAST STRAIN	AMT.

OTHER INGREDIENTS	AMT.

BREWING					
TIME	STEP	[STRIKE, MASH-IN, MASH-OUT, SPARGE, BOIL, KNOCKOUT]	TEMP	VOLUME	GRAVITY
	1.				
	2.				
	3.				
	4.				
	5.				
	6.				

FERMENTATION					
DATE	STEP		START TEMP	END TEMP	GRAVITY	DAYS
	1.				
	2.				
	3.				
	4.				

FERMENTATION ADDITIONS

DATE	ADDITION	AMT.	DAYS

PACKAGING

DATE	FINAL VOLUME	NUMBER OF BOTTLES	NUMBER OF KEGS	READY TO DRINK BY DATE

INGREDIENTS INFORMATION

....
....
....
....
....
....
....

BREWING NOTES

....
....
....
....
....
....
....

TASTING NOTES

ADDITIONAL INFORMATION

UNITS OF MEASUREMENT	
TEMP	
WEIGHT	
VOLUME	

BEER INFO

RATING: ☆ ☆ ☆ ☆ ☆

BEER NAME .... BATCH NO. ....

STYLE .... BATCH VOLUME ....

BREWER .... DATE ....

OG		FG		ABV		SRM		IBU	
EXPECTED	ACTUAL								

GRAIN	AMT.
TOTAL	

HOPS		FORM	AA	IBU	TIME	AMT.
		TOTAL				

WATER TREATMENTS	pH		AMT.

YEAST STRAIN	AMT.

OTHER INGREDIENTS	AMT.

BREWING

TIME	STEP [STRIKE, MASH-IN, MASH-OUT, SPARGE, BOIL, KNOCKOUT]	TEMP	VOLUME	GRAVITY
	1.			
	2.			
	3.			
	4.			
	5.			
	6.			

FERMENTATION

DATE	STEP	START TEMP	END TEMP	GRAVITY	DAYS
	1.				
	2.				
	3.				
	4.				

FERMENTATION ADDITIONS

DATE	ADDITION	AMT.	DAYS

PACKAGING

DATE	FINAL VOLUME	NUMBER OF BOTTLES	NUMBER OF KEGS	READY TO DRINK BY DATE

INGREDIENTS INFORMATION

....
....
....
....
....
....
....

BREWING NOTES

....
....
....
....
....
....
....

TASTING NOTES

ADDITIONAL INFORMATION

UNITS OF MEASUREMENT	
TEMP	
WEIGHT	
VOLUME	

BEER INFO		RATING: ☆ ☆ ☆ ☆ ☆

BEER NAME .... BATCH NO. ....

STYLE .... BATCH VOLUME ....

BREWER .... DATE ....

OG		FG		ABV		SRM		IBU	
EXPECTED	ACTUAL								

GRAIN	AMT.
TOTAL	

HOPS	FORM	AA	IBU	TIME	AMT.
TOTAL					

WATER TREATMENTS	pH		AMT.

YEAST STRAIN	AMT.

OTHER INGREDIENTS	AMT.

BREWING					
TIME	STEP [STRIKE, MASH-IN, MASH-OUT, SPARGE, BOIL, KNOCKOUT]		TEMP	VOLUME	GRAVITY
	1.				
	2.				
	3.				
	4.				
	5.				
	6.				

FERMENTATION					
DATE	STEP	START TEMP	END TEMP	GRAVITY	DAYS
	1.				
	2.				
	3.				
	4.				

FERMENTATION ADDITIONS

DATE	ADDITION	AMT.	DAYS

PACKAGING

DATE	FINAL VOLUME	NUMBER OF BOTTLES	NUMBER OF KEGS	READY TO DRINK BY DATE

INGREDIENTS INFORMATION

....
....
....
....
....
....
....

BREWING NOTES

....
....
....
....
....
....
....

TASTING NOTES

ADDITIONAL INFORMATION

UNITS OF MEASUREMENT	
TEMP	
WEIGHT	
VOLUME	

| BEER INFO | | | | | RATING: | ☆ ☆ ☆ ☆ ☆ |

BEER NAME .... **BATCH NO.** ....

STYLE .... **BATCH VOLUME** ....

BREWER .... **DATE** ....

OG		FG		ABV		SRM		IBU	
EXPECTED	ACTUAL								

GRAIN	AMT.
TOTAL	

HOPS	FORM	AA	IBU	TIME	AMT.
TOTAL					

WATER TREATMENTS	pH		AMT.

YEAST STRAIN	AMT.

OTHER INGREDIENTS	AMT.

BREWING					
TIME	**STEP** [STRIKE, MASH-IN, MASH-OUT, SPARGE, BOIL, KNOCKOUT]		**TEMP**	**VOLUME**	**GRAVITY**
	1.				
	2.				
	3.				
	4.				
	5.				
	6.				

FERMENTATION					
DATE	**STEP**	**START TEMP**	**END TEMP**	**GRAVITY**	**DAYS**
	1.				
	2.				
	3.				
	4.				

FERMENTATION ADDITIONS

DATE	ADDITION	AMT.	DAYS

PACKAGING

DATE	FINAL VOLUME	NUMBER OF BOTTLES	NUMBER OF KEGS	READY TO DRINK BY DATE

INGREDIENTS INFORMATION

....
....
....
....
....
....
....

BREWING NOTES

....
....
....
....
....
....
....

TASTING NOTES

ADDITIONAL INFORMATION

UNITS OF MEASUREMENT	
TEMP	
WEIGHT	
VOLUME	

BEER INFO

RATING: ☆ ☆ ☆ ☆ ☆

BEER NAME .... BATCH NO. ....

STYLE .... BATCH VOLUME ....

BREWER .... DATE ....

OG		FG		ABV		SRM		IBU	
EXPECTED	ACTUAL								

GRAIN	AMT.
TOTAL	

HOPS	FORM	AA	IBU	TIME	AMT.
TOTAL					

WATER TREATMENTS	pH		AMT.

YEAST STRAIN	AMT.

OTHER INGREDIENTS	AMT.

BREWING

TIME	STEP [STRIKE, MASH-IN, MASH-OUT, SPARGE, BOIL, KNOCKOUT]	TEMP	VOLUME	GRAVITY
	1.			
	2.			
	3.			
	4.			
	5.			
	6.			

FERMENTATION

DATE	STEP	START TEMP	END TEMP	GRAVITY	DAYS
	1.				
	2.				
	3.				
	4.				

FERMENTATION ADDITIONS

DATE	ADDITION	AMT.	DAYS

PACKAGING

DATE	FINAL VOLUME	NUMBER OF BOTTLES	NUMBER OF KEGS	READY TO DRINK BY DATE

INGREDIENTS INFORMATION

....

....

....

....

....

....

....

BREWING NOTES

....

....

....

....

....

....

....

TASTING NOTES

ADDITIONAL INFORMATION

UNITS OF MEASUREMENT	
TEMP	
WEIGHT	
VOLUME	

BEER INFO	RATING:	☆ ☆ ☆ ☆ ☆

BEER NAME .... **BATCH NO.** ....

STYLE .... **BATCH VOLUME** ....

BREWER .... **DATE** ....

OG		FG		ABV		SRM		IBU	
EXPECTED	ACTUAL								

GRAIN	AMT.
TOTAL	

HOPS	FORM	AA	IBU	TIME	AMT.
TOTAL					

WATER TREATMENTS	pH		AMT.

YEAST STRAIN	AMT.

OTHER INGREDIENTS	AMT.

BREWING					
TIME	STEP	[STRIKE, MASH-IN, MASH-OUT, SPARGE, BOIL, KNOCKOUT]	TEMP	VOLUME	GRAVITY
	1.				
	2.				
	3.				
	4.				
	5.				
	6.				

FERMENTATION					
DATE	STEP		START TEMP	END TEMP	GRAVITY	DAYS
	1.				
	2.				
	3.				
	4.				

FERMENTATION ADDITIONS

DATE	ADDITION	AMT.	DAYS

PACKAGING

DATE	FINAL VOLUME	NUMBER OF BOTTLES	NUMBER OF KEGS	READY TO DRINK BY DATE

INGREDIENTS INFORMATION

....
....
....
....
....
....
....

BREWING NOTES

....
....
....
....
....
....
....

TASTING NOTES

ADDITIONAL INFORMATION

UNITS OF MEASUREMENT	
TEMP	
WEIGHT	
VOLUME	

| BEER INFO | | | | | | | RATING: | ☆ | ☆ | ☆ | ☆ | ☆ |

BEER NAME .... BATCH NO. ....

STYLE .... BATCH VOLUME ....

BREWER .... DATE ....

OG		FG		ABV		SRM		IBU	
EXPECTED	ACTUAL								

GRAIN	AMT.
TOTAL	

HOPS	FORM	AA	IBU	TIME	AMT.
TOTAL					

WATER TREATMENTS	pH		AMT.

YEAST STRAIN	AMT.

OTHER INGREDIENTS	AMT.

BREWING					
TIME	STEP	[STRIKE, MASH-IN, MASH-OUT, SPARGE, BOIL, KNOCKOUT]	TEMP	VOLUME	GRAVITY
	1.				
	2.				
	3.				
	4.				
	5.				
	6.				

FERMENTATION					
DATE	STEP		START TEMP	END TEMP	GRAVITY	DAYS
	1.					
	2.					
	3.					
	4.					

FERMENTATION ADDITIONS

DATE	ADDITION	AMT.	DAYS

PACKAGING

DATE	FINAL VOLUME	NUMBER OF BOTTLES	NUMBER OF KEGS	READY TO DRINK BY DATE

INGREDIENTS INFORMATION

....
....
....
....
....
....
....

BREWING NOTES

....
....
....
....
....
....
....

TASTING NOTES

ADDITIONAL INFORMATION

UNITS OF MEASUREMENT	
TEMP	
WEIGHT	
VOLUME	

Made in the USA
Coppell, TX
07 December 2020